ODE
TO
THE
PUNANI

ODE TO THE PUNANI: SENSUAL RISING

Written By: Sharran C. Taylor
A.K.A. Kween Yakini

Editor: Christina K. Taylor

Cover Design: Sharran C. Taylor

Other Books by Sharran C. Taylor

WOKE: A POETIC JOURNEY

KWEEN
YAKINI

amazon.com/author/sharrantaylor

Copyright © 2016, 2017, 2018, 2019

By Sharran C. Taylor

ISBN: 978-1-7323710-2-6

This is a work of fiction. The names, characters, places and incidents are products of the writer's imagination or have been used fictitiously and are not to be constructed as real. Any resemblance to persons, living or deceased, actual events, locales or organizations is entirely coincidental.

TABLE OF CONTENTS

PUNANI EDIFICATION

ODE TO THE PUNANI....................................8

A YOUNG MAN'S GOTTA LEARN....................11

SWEET SADIE..14

FUCK BOY..17

I'M THE GLITCH IN YOUR MATRIX.................20

LOVING HIM COMPLETELY..........................24

SOULS SPEAKING.....................................27

HOT IN THE KITCHEN................................30

THE ALL WOMAN 3000..............................34

THE APHRODISIAC....................................36

PUNANI DEVOTION

YONI WORSHIP...40

TAKEN...42

LOVE LIKE A SIN......................................44

LOVE OF MY LIFE.....................................49

SACRED FRUIT...51

THE AFRICAN BUSH..................................54

THE PUSSY ANTHEM SONG........................58

SLAY THE PUNANI

FREAKIEST DESIRE...........................62

SEX SLAVE....................................65

MR. KRYPTONITE..............................68

I WANT THAT Oooooo Weeeee............73

I'M SHOOK....................................76

THE WOMAN CONNOISSEUR..............79

MY DARK KNIGHT.............................81

MINDGASMS...................................84

THE PUNANI ZONE

SEXY AND GROWN.............................88

THE HONEYMOON..............................91

ANTICIPATING................................94

CAPTURING HIS ESSENCE...................97

RIDEM COWGIRL...............................100

THAT DUDE....................................102

PUNANI PLAYDATES

I NEED A FREAK…………………………………108

WANTING HIM…………………………………..112

G-SPOT…………………………………………...115

BLACK OASIS……………………………………118

INVITED………………………………………….121

SEXUAL BEAST………………………......123

THE-HIT-IT-MAN………………………………127

SOME NIGHTS………………………........131

BOOK PREVIEW……………………………….135

ACKNOWLEDGEMENT

I am so grateful for everyone who has encouraged me to pursue my passion for writing. I'm especially thankful for my daughter Christina who has been my biggest supporter of all, and her editing work on this project has made my work shine even brighter. She is invaluable to me, and I'm so blessed to have her as my daughter.

INTRODUCTION

RED INK

This erotica is so hot!
That it should be written in red ink

I bet this "Ode to the Punani"

Gone have you thirsty for a drink

Don't you wanna nibble on this cookie

I promise you're gone love this nookie

Gonna have you saying

Awww, sookie, sookie!

And leave you blushing like rookie

Yeah, I'm really quite nasty

But I still know how to keep it classy

I can't be held by no chastity

And only a freak can get at me

But I'll never kiss and tell

I'll just seduce you with a spell

Lubricate your mind like a gel

Then let you slide deep inside my well

I can tease you like a vixen

Have you holding crystals like a wiccan
Put you in a horny condition
And leave your orifice dripping
I wanna leave your mind full not hollow
Just sip me slow like a nice Moscato
But make sure you swallow
Before I hit you with this bravado

It's time for some adult conversation
So, cum and get this mental penetration
I'll make you tingle with elation
And definitely raise your vibration

Cause this erotica is so hot!
That it should be written in red ink
I bet this "Ode to the Punani"
Gone have you thirsty for a drink
Don't you wanna nibble on this cookie
I promise you gone love this nookie
Gonna have you saying
Awww, sookie, sookie!
And leave you blushing like rookie

PUNANI
EDIFICATION

ODE TO THE PUNANI

I am the punani
And the punani is she
Because I am her
And she is me
Yeah I bet you ain't never had none
This good
This sensual
Or this hood
So, let this "Ode To The Punani"
Make my powers understood

I bet you ain't never moaned this much
I bet you ain't never penetrated this gut
I bet you love the way my Kegels
Is giving you the greatest nut

If you worship me like a Queen
I'll make all your dreams come true
But if you disrespect my punani
Then I'll leave them balls sad and blue
Because I desire one who is worthy
And one who is strong not weak

I value loyalty above all else
And I disregard those who cheat

I have the nature of a Goddess
That's why I'm naturally protective
And when it's time to choose a mate
I can be very selective

I'm the reason he grinds to make that money
I am the land of milk and honey
I am man's greatest gift
I am the reason why he licks his lips
I am the taste on the tip of his tongue
I am the air inside his lungs
I am the ocean to his wave
I am the one he truly craves

They may try to seduce me
Pleading at my doors
Thinking they can tame me
With their oh so mighty roars
Yet one, by one
They'll try and they will yearn
But this "Ode To The Punani"
Will be a lesson they must learn

Because the punani is man's first home
The place where he sprang
From my sacred catacomb
That's why he finds my energy so
Alluring and provoking
Because this sugary sweet nectar was
Perfectly made to ease his stroking

That's why I am the punani
And the punani is she
Because I am her
And she is me
I can tell you ain't never had none
This good
This sensual
Or this hood
So, let this "Ode to The Punani"
Make my powers understood!

A YOUNG MAN'S GOTTA LEARN

Now, you know what they say
They say that a Young Man has got to learn
And who better to teach him then me…

Well, my, my, young man
What do we have here?
Won't you come a little bit closer
So, I can kick this in your ear

Yes, I am a little bit older
But please have no fear
Cause I'm just trying to
Elevate your mind my dear

Yes, I may be more mature
But I still remember how to play
And baby when it comes to good dick
I don't run away
I Slay!
And you are just my type
Young, dark and sexy
With a long pipe

Yes indeed, you've got what I want
But the question is
Can you handle this
Grown woman's cunt?

My, My, Young Man
I don't mean to be rude
But I see his head is starting to protrude
I think he might be in the mood
And what I want to know is
How deep can you go?
I mean is it a Short Ride
Or is it a long Mandingo?

Please excuse me young man
I don't mean to give you such a speech
But oh, my goodness!
What size are those feet?
Now you know what they say
About a man with big feet
They say that the bigger they are
The further he can reach

Now I'm no expert
But I know how to make this punani twerk

So, be careful young man
That you don't get hurt
Cause I'm the type of woman
Who's not afraid to put in the work

I can make this punani squeeze
That dick so hard
You'll be saying oh my god
When I start to slide down on that rod

So, why don't we do a little
Something, something
Let's get bumping!
Cause I wanna ride you like swing
And do some pumping

Young man, young man
Tonight, I've got big plans!
And I can't wait!
To wrap your dick inside my hands!
I'm gone make you stand
Like a stick in the sand
And before this night is through
I promise you'll be a grown ass man!

SWEET SADIE

Now girl check him out!
That brotha is fine as dark molasses!
Wait a minute now!
Let me put on my glasses!
Hm, hm, hm, hey baby
Who am I?
Well they call me Sweet Sadie
Cause I'm the around the way girl
And put it down kind of lady
And you sho is fine mister
You got me feeling a little crazy
And if I was just a little bit younger
I might wanna have your baby
Because all I need is a taste
Of your delicious gravy
And I'm heading straight to the moon
And that ain't no if's, and's, but's
or maybe's

Now I'm gone give you this lovin for free
Cause usually I make them pay me
You see I'm a hustler baby

And there ain't nothing about me lazy

But yo type of sexiness

Got me wanting to do some

"Dirty Dancing" like "Patrick Swayze"

Yeah, my Dunkin Hines cake

Might leave your face a little glazy

And after a few nights with me

That headboard might get a little shaky

But I'll give you a little break

So, you can stop and smell the daisies

Though I must admit your cologne

Got me feeling kind of racy

And I'm not like them young girls

Talking about "what have you done for me lately"?

Because all I wanna do is

Shake what my mamma gave me

Cause you see Sweet Sadie

Is an old school kind of lady

Yeah, I like that R&B music

From the nineties and the eighties

When we use to tell the D.J.

Just "Turn off the lights"

And let Teddy Pendergrass take me

So, don't worry boo because I got you

And I'll never act flaky

Unless you try to hit it and forsake me

Then you might catch these hands

Cause that's how my mama raised me

So, honey now you know why

They call me Sweet Sadie

Cause I'm the around the way girl

And put it down kind of lady

And you sho is fine mister

You got me feeling a kind of crazy

Because if I was a just little bit younger

I might wanna have your baby

And all I really need is a taste

Of your delicious gravy

And I'm heading straight to the moon

And that ain't no if's, and's, but's

or maybe's

FUCKBOY

What's that you say boy?

Oh, you just a fuck boy

But guess what boy?

This is Jamaican Rum pussy boy

This pussy will leave you numb boy

I think you better run boy

Cause you're just a fuck boy

A side dick toy

So, don't even try to play me boy

Cause I'm through with all these fuck boys

So, don't try your luck boy

Cause you just a rubber dub duck boy

A quick fuck in the tub boy!

And you can't bring this pussy joy

Cause this is grown pussy boy

This kind of pussy starts wars

Like Helen of Troy

This is tsunami pussy boy

It only takes a second

And my Kegels deploy

You better listen Boy!

Because I'll swallow that dick up like a void

What's that you say boy?
Hmm, now don't push your luck boy
Cause you just a play toy
Thinking you a playboy
And if I slay that dick boy
That mind I'll destroy!
And leave that community dick unemployed

Well I'm just saying boy
Now don't get up in your feeling's boy
Because I know your dick just be a decoy
And you just a come through boy
And a ride-um toy
I know you're no real McCoy
Do you hear me boy?

Because you're slacking boy
And I don't care if packing boy
So, just keep jacking boy!

And let me say this boy

This is Jamaican rum pussy boy

This pussy will leave you numb boy

So, I think you better run boy

Cause you're just a fuck boy

And I'm through with all these fuck boys!

I'M THE GLITCH IN YOUR MATRIX

Don't you know who I am?

I am the Glitch in your matrix

And you need me

As much as I need you

And it's not just that I need you

Cause when I'm sexing you, I feed you

And when I feed you, I'm sexing you

Don't you get it?

I'm the Source

And you need me to stay alive

Or at least make you feel like you're living

Because I am the light

And life is what I'm giving!

So, let me expand your vision

So, I can upgrade your system

And improve the flow of your algorithm

Yes, I'll be your technician

So, that we can get in the right position

Then you can key stroke my body

With accurate precision

Now we can proceed with the right formation

Because you have effectively stimulated my lubrication

Allowing us to enjoy a deeper penetration

So, that we can climax at a higher elevation

But what you are detecting

Is a stronger internal connection

Because now you can feel my Kegels flexing

On the tip of your erection

And when you give me your warm injections

I'll carry our seed with the utmost protection

Yeah, I know you gotta have it

I know you wanna hit it like a savage

And ride me like a carriage

Cause my sex is way above the average

That's why I got ya mind ravaged

By the alchemy of this marriage

But tell me where do you end?

And where do I begin?

Because this sex way too metaphysical

For this to be a sin

Yes, you are correct

This is more than just good sex

Indeed, this is the way
We're supposed to connect
This ritual was designed by the creator
Who we call the Architect

So, now it's time to reach our greatness
And together we'll build a new matrix
Cause I'm your beloved Trinity
And you are my Neo let's face it!

Yes, you are my one
The chosen Son
And no one can erase this
So, if this is our new reality
Then I'm the glitch in your matrix

So, now do you understand?
That you need me
As much as I need you
And it's not just that I need you
Cause when I'm sexing you, I feed you
And when I feed you, I'm sexing you
Don't you Get it?

I'm the Source

And you need me to stay alive

Or at least, make you feel like you're living

Because I am the light

And life is what I'm giving!

LOVING HIM COMPLETELY

First, she kissed his forehead
The home of his noble Third Eye
Because that's the place where consciousness occurs
A place that allows him to see her
Beyond this physical plane
Loving him completely

Second, she kissed his eyelids
The place where his dreams and desires dwell
The place where his most erotic thoughts are conceived
Loving him completely

Then, she moved down further to kiss his soft lips
For this is the place where he speaks to her heart
The place where he speaks of his love and devotion
Loving him completely

Then she kissed his neck which is the doorway to his
passion
Igniting his erogenous spot
Leading him to the place where he surrenders
And gives into the moment

Loving him completely

Now she trails her tongue down his chest
Greeting his masculine energy
With her seductive pheromones
Skillfully caressing and massaging him
She wets his nipples with her warm tongue
Provoking his well-endowed erection
Loving him completely

Then she follows him
As he inhales and exhales
Breathing to his rhythm
While slowly moving down
Down pass his firm abdominals
As her wet tongue leads the way
He holds his breath in anticipation
Loving him completely

She pauses at the arrival of her destination
She salivates imagining his essence on her tongue
Abundantly dripping from her lips
Because she is more than ready to feast on his sensuality
She licks her lips relishing the taste of him
Now they are both ready

Loving him completely

Ferociously she swallows him
Relaxing her mouth around his flesh
So that she can savor all of him
Blissfulness is achieved
As she drinks his warm nectar
Releasing profound pleasures
Knowing the depths of her love for him
He moans with pure contentment
Because she loved him completely

SOULS SPEAKING

Our souls are speaking

Can't you hear those desires

Calling and roaring

That sensual energy is soaring

Hear it swishing and hissing

Because we know something's missing

You see, our souls are speaking

Just listen!

I think it's time

For some slow wet kissing

Feels like we need to get

Some essence dripping

We need a Yoni whipping

So, let's change positions

Because these satin sheets keep slipping

And if you keep on hard hitting

There's gone be some mattress flipping

Because our souls are speaking

Just listen!

While your mind is sleeping

Our souls be late night-creeping

Lust-seeking

Beds-squeaking

Curse words bleeping

And holy tongue speaking

We need more caressing

Need to feel pelvic bones pressing

When I'm slowly undressing

It keeps your spirit obsessing

Cause when I see your erection

Oh, what a blessing!

You see our souls are speaking

Just listen!

Feels like we're imploding

I think our DNA is encoding

I see your phallus your reloading

But you better hurry up

Because this shop is soon closing

Why do we look up at the stars gazing?

Why do we give up praise?

But still be hell raising?

Are we just going through phases?

Or are we just chasing this high
Because it feels so amazing

I think we need a spiritual advisor
We need a divine energizer
We need to become wiser
But if you want me to open my legs wider
Then you need to become a full sizer
So that I can become a good rider

Cause our souls just be drifting
In and out of dimensions
Our souls just be shifting
Flowing through the wind
You can hear our desires twisting
Because our souls are speaking
Just listen!

HOT IN THE KITCHEN

I invited this fine Chef

To come and cook in my kitchen

He said that he wanted to show me everything

That I had been missing

Well I got so damn tickled

When he told me about the size of that pickle

That I wanted to let out a big cheer

Because I was getting a little parched

And he was looking like a tall glass of Root Beer

Somehow, I knew that he was gonna be

A real good packer

Cause he seemed like the type of Brotha

Who knew how to butter a lady's cracker

So, I said I sure do hope that you don't take

this the wrong way

But I would love to get a sample

Of your chocolate soufflé

So, he told me it felt like his Butter Finger

was getting stiff

Because my chocolate ganache was looking so thick

So, I told him I'll give you a little sample

Go ahead and put some on the tip

He told me that sometimes his Almond Joy

needs a few nuts

But sometimes it could just use one

I said well ok Mr. Good Bar

I see that cooking with you is gonna be a lot fun

But I must admit this is a nice treat

Although I have never had this much food to eat

So, I hope you enjoy eating my sweets

I think I better make some more sauce

For all that meat

Chef, I'm so glad to have you in my home

So, I'll let you filet my fish

While I put some marinade

On your T-bone

I could feel the temperature getting hot

Inside my kitchen

Girl, he was showing me everything

That I had been missing

So, I asked if he preferred breast, legs, or thighs

I want to taste it all was how he replied!

His meat was real thick

So, I cooked it nice and slow

Until all those juices started to flow

But he noticed how I kept licking my lips

So, he offered me some of his milk

And it slid right down my throat

Just as smooth as silk

I liked the way he poured his cream into my pot

And the way it kept rising

And rising all the way to the top

Cause he wasn't the type

To just slide his hot dog inside my bun

He went through everything in my kitchen

before we were done

He gave me some of his salty chips

And I gave him some of my creamy dip

He asked me if I wanted my salad tossed

So, I gave him a wink

And said you cook like a Boss!

Girl, he ate so many of my cookies

I started calling him the cookie monster

Then he looked up and smiled at me

And said that my seafood tasted better than Red Lobsters

And before he left

He grabbed some more of my fruits

And told me that he wanted one more sample

Of my Caribbean Island juice

Then I said thank you for coming

I sure did enjoy the flavor of your meat

He said let's do it again real soon

Because I thoroughly enjoyed eating your sweets

Girl, that man really knew his way

Around the kitchen!

And I learned quite a few tips

About all the things that were missing

THE ALL WOMAN 3000

Greetings shoppers!
In this dynamic year of 2025
Allow me to introduce to you
Our latest work of art
Here is our Cybernetic Advance
Prototype All Woman 3000
This model is designed to give life enhancing sex

It doesn't matter if you like to cum fast
or take your time and make it last
This model will never leave you with regrets
Our most popular dimensions are
36 - 24 – 36

She can take endless grinding
She was made to stay wet
She comes in all shades
When you place your order
You can take your pick
You'll get lost inside her
Full welcoming lips
She can be intimately configured

To accommodate any size dick
And her advanced programming
Can give your cock the most pleasing tricks

No matter how deep you go
She'll never say stop or it hurts
We can make her moan and vibrate
We can make even make her twerk

So, shoppers if you need an erotic doll
That's guaranteed to fit
Then our Prototype All Woman 3000
 Is going to be the perfect gift!

THE APHRODISIAC

The Aphrodisiac
Has got what your relationship needs
So, enjoy this erotic therapy
Cum and let your bodies feed
Cause I'm about to raise your libidos
To their highest speed
But first I wanna hear you say
Thank you please!

Now if you learn these skills
She'll stop acting so mean
The next time she's cussing and fussing
Just go down on your knees

Fulfill both of your desires
And your erotic dreams
If you learn to eat that punani right
You're sure to make her scream

She needs for you to devour that pussy
Smother her clit in whipped cream
Because love making is a sport

So, I'm here to help you make the team

Now offer her a glass of champagne
With some sliced strawberry's
While you lick chocolate off her nipples
And suck on that sweet fat cherry

Now if she wanna give you some head
But your size might make her choke
Then try a tablespoon of honey
To gently coat the back of her throat

Now sit back and enjoy that head
Let her lick on your balls
And I bet that punani gone be wetter
Then the rivers of Niagara Falls

You may need to swallow a few oysters
To put some intensity back in your stroke
I do hope you're paying attention
I hope your taking some notes

Congrats you made the team
Now get yo ass up off the bench
And give her all that good dick

Inch by glorious inch

You never cum before she does
So, hold that nut Mr. Grinch
You better slow down your stroke
She can feel you starting to flinch

Now it's time to pull out and cum
Because that punani is drenched
Then go down and lick every delicious drop
Until your thirst is thoroughly quenched

You can even eat it from the back
I bet the freak in her likes that shit
Or hold them sexy legs down
And softly suck on that fat juicy clit

Now there's less frustration
Because that punani was lit
So, the next time she's cussing you out
Just go down and scratch that itch!

PUNANI DEVOTION

YONI WORSHIP

She descended into a blissful state
As her essence began to swell
And her body yearned for more and more
Of his satisfyingly sensual spell

She appreciated his technique
And she admired the intensity of his application
She enjoyed the way he quenched her fire
With such fierce determination
Indeed, her Yoni was pleased
With his oral stimulation
Cause he knew how to worship that Yoni
And he'd won her complete admiration

He unabashedly moaned as he gorged
on her delectable nectar
Because she was truly the giver
And he was happy to be the collector
His tongue probed inside her
Commanding her full attention
While she swooned and swayed
On his tongue's penetration

And never before had her Yoni

Reached this realm of gratification

She noticed how he devoured every drop

Of her sweet condensation

He granted her with so many orgasms

That her Yoni felt slightly numb

Leaving her to curiously ponder

How many times had she cum?

So, he gently kissed her sweet clit

Because tasting her Yoni was a

Rewarding treasure

And then he whispered you're welcome my love

Eating you has truly been my pleasure

TAKEN

He took me,
He took me to the edge of my inhibitions
Then released me into a pool of ecstasy
It was more than just a fantasy
Now my curiosity has got the best of me
He took me

He took me to the new land of nothing forbidden
He taught me how to master my rhythm
Always kept it 100
No secrets hidden
He took me

He took me to the place
Where hot oils spilled
It smelled like daffodils
There were too many thrills
You made me submit to your will
You had me shaking from pleasure until
You left my body still
He took me

He took me up to my peak

Made me unleash my inner freak

I could barely speak!

He took me

He took me

Damn he took me

I'm taken!

LOVE LIKE A SIN

Miss, I didn't mean to stare
So, please excuse me!
But, have we met somewhere before?
Because your vibe just threw me
If wanting to lick your pussy is a Sin
Well just go ahead and sue me
Because I wanna take you on
Long romantic trips
Fuck dinner and a movie!

For far too long I've waited for you
So, tell me where you have been
Cause I'm sure that there is nothing sweeter
Then the taste of your honey brown skin
And I just can't wait to get high
On that warm delicious gin
Because pussy that tastes that good
has got to be a sin!

King Nahjan is my name
Sexual healing is my aim
But I think I just found my soulmate

Because your beauty is now etched
On the interior of my brain
I swear I'm keeping it real
I'm too old for those games
And I'm gonna make it my mission
To quench every bit of that flame

I'll give you quality time
We can stroll through the mall
Because I want your mind and your body
I wanna have it all
I wanna come inside
And knock down those walls
Cause I can see a whole lotta orgasms
For you in my crystal ball!

And sweetheart I'm not joking
Because I know you been
Waiting and hoping
For some exceptional stroking
That will leave the sheets soaking
And have them detectors smoking

That's why my dick is the perfect verb
And your pussy is the proper noun

Plus, I know that whatever I put in your gut

Is gonna come back down

Queen, I'll be licking that pussy

From Sunup to Sundown

Leave your legs shaking so hard

You'll be screaming without a sound

Baby you need a king to satisfy that pussy

One who will also give honor

And respect to your crown

So, let me uplift your body and soul

And let that delicious love cum down

So, just lay back on that pillow

And keep them sexy legs open

Let me surf through your waves

And get to know the rhythm of your ocean

Cause I can't wait to hear you scream

When that climax is approaching

And once that pussy gets wet

I'm gone stroke you hard in slow motion!

Let every intimate thrust

Take your emotions higher

No, I'm not a religious man

But it feels like I'm
Preaching to the choir
And now that I'm your King
Just call me your Sire
Because whatever you crave
Will be my greatest desire

I'll run your bath water
And help you undress '
I'll rub that body down
And eliminate any stress

So, when you want that pussy licked
There's no need to be shy
Just put my head between your thighs
And let me feast on that pie

Cause this long fat tongue
Can do some serious tricks
And once I feast on that delicious clit
I promise my wood is gonna be standing stiff

I wanna get that pussy dripping wet
So, you can slide up and down on my pole
Makes me wanna bathe in your essence

And let it cleanse my soul

Because, for far too long I've waited for you
So, tell me where you've been
Cause I'm sure that there is nothing sweeter
Then the taste of your honey brown skin

And I just can't wait to get high
On that delicious gin
Because pussy that taste this good
has got to be a Sin!

LOVE OF MY LIFE

Sometimes I feel like
I just want to play in it
But when it gets real good
I just want to lay in it
I gotta go to work
So, I just can't stay in it
But I'm wishing I could spend
The whole got damn day in it!

Baby I'm loving this feeling
I feel like I can fly
The deepness inside
Is transforming my mind
You have shown me your light
So, now I'm no longer blind
This is the greatest pleasure on earth
Damn, I'm so lucky to find
Baby hold me!
Catch me!
Can't you see me falling?
I can't stop moaning your name
Can't you hear me calling?

I keep playing back this feeling
I am forever recalling
Baby your love is so perfect
So, there is no need for stalling

You've elevated my consciousness
And you've taken me higher!
You've stirred up my soul
And made it catch on fire!
Now I can't seem to fight this growing desire
Because I'm so gone in your love
Baby I'm ready to retire!

So, now I'm never letting go!
Baby I'm willing to fight
And I'm ready to give you my heart
Your love is worth any price
Your punani is gripping me hard
Oooh it feels just right!
Baby I'm gonna stay in this love
For the rest of my life!

SACRED FRUIT

Her sacred fruit is a favor from god

The healing power of her nectar

is not a myth

And very few are worthy to receive

Her magnificent and heavenly gifts

Yes, her proverbial cherry

Is an eternal habit-forming bliss

So, come and reap the harvest

That blooms between her bountiful hips

Behold, her plump and succulent berry

Is yearning to be picked!

Come feast on her sacred fruit

It's ripe and ready for your lips!

Always be her protector

And she'll nourish you

With sweet precipitation

Always be honest and loyal

And that will suffice as compensation

Because the sacred fruit of a goddess

Is simply one of a kind

It is something to be treasured
For her nectar is truly divine
Quickly you'll become addicted
And get inebriated from her wine
So, think before you pick her
Cause believe me that's no lie

You'll be craving her sweet essence
Begging to have her again and again
So, come and experience this wonder
Because this is where man's paradise begins

Enjoy the sacred fruit from god
The healing power of her nectar
is not just a myth
And very few are worthy to receive
Her magnificent and heavenly gifts
Yes, her proverbial cherry
Is an eternal habit-forming bliss
So, come and reap the harvest
That blooms between her
bountiful hips
Behold her plump and succulent berry
Is yearning to be picked!
So, come and be blessed

Her sacred fruit is ripe
And ready for your lips!

AFRICAN BUSH

I hope you got that good dick
I hope you can hang with me
Cause I swear my punani is so amazing
Darling they ain't even got a name for me!

Can you do whatever it takes?
Can you leave my pussy shook?
Have I finally found a man
Who can tame my African Bush?
Cause she ain't nothing like
That old regular puss
You see this right here
Be that savage Kush!

She's so addictive
That she really should come with a warning
Cause I can make that dick cum so hard
I'll have it brain storming

My bush has a mind of her own
She desire's it all
She wants every bit of that dick

All the way down to your balls

So, I hope you've got the kind of wood
That keeps her yearning
The kind of wood that's so good
It just keeps on serving and serving
She wants that dick so good
It's seems incomprehensible
Can you make this pussy astral project?
Like it's multi-dimensional

Because this punani is a gift
So, you gotta slowly unwrap it
Then sign your name on my clit
I wanna feel you autograph it
Go ahead take your time
No need to rush it
If she feels too good on your head
Then your stroke might need
Some adjusting

Can you make this kitty talk?
Let me see you face it
My nectar is like pineapples and mangos
You know you wanna taste it

Ooh stop right there
And just let your tongue trace it
My legs are shaking
But don't stop because I can take it
Baby just stay focused
And let your mind embrace it
Bravo, bravo!
Yeah, I think we gonna make it!

Push me up against the wall
Then bend me over on the couch
Make me cum so hard
That you erase all my doubts

Honey I'll do whatever it takes
To make that dick smile
Pull my legs over my head
You know I'm versatile
We can do it missionary
Or doggy style
My pussy is in the home stretch
Cause your dick went the extra mile

Now I see you'll do whatever it takes
Cause you got this pussy Shook!

I'm so glad I finally found a man
Who can tame this African Bush!
Cause she ain't nothing like
That old regular puss
I told you this right here
Be that Savage Kush

Honey that dick was exceptional
And there ain't many who can hang with me
Cause this punani is so amazing
Sweetie they ain't even got a name for me

THE PUSSY ANTHEM SONG

It's that Ooooooo Aaaaaah
Can I get it from the side?
It's that Ooooooo Aaaaaah
The cream fillings inside
It's that Ooooooo Aaaaaah
This pussy might leave you blind
It's that Ooooooo Aaaaaah
This pussy one of a kind!

You better come get it!
Better spit it
Before you hit it
Stop playing
Don't Quit it!
Hold up
I can split it
If you wit it
Hmmm

It's that yeah what
I see you looking at my butt!
It's that yeah what
And you know I like to fuck!

It's that yeah what
You better hold that nut!
It's that yeah what
Can you get it in my gut?

Yo dick be
Unleashing!
G-spot reaching!
What you teaching?
When we're freaking
You Got me
Dirty speaking
Now I'm leaking
Cause I'm peaking!

Ooooooo Aaaaaah!
Can I get it from the side?
It's that Ooooooo Aaaaaah!
The cream fillings inside
It's that Ooooooo Aaaaaah!
This pussy might leave you blind
It's that Ooooooo Aaaaaah!
This pussy one of a kind

It's that oh damn!

Fuck here we go again
It's that oh Damn!
I got that sweetest honey yam
It's that oh damn!
I'll make that long dick stand
It's that oh damn!
Now shoot that vi-de-o cam

It's that Aww shit!
I feel you sucking on my tits
It's that Aww shit!
Can you lick around my clit?
It's that Aww shit!
You got me do back flips
It's that Aww shit!
How long is that dick!

It's that Ooooooo Aaaaaah!
Can I get it from the side?
It's that Ooooooo Aaaaaah!
The cream fillings inside
It's that Ooooooo Aaaaaah!
This pussy might leave you blind
It's that Ooooooo Aaaaaah!
This pussy one of a kind!

SLAY
THE
PUNANI

FREAKIEST DESIRE

Damn it feels like I'm caught up
In some freaky tailspin
But I just wanna see the flexibility
Of those sexy long limbs
I just wanna give you this yang
So, I can suck on that phat yin
Let me take you to my bedroom
So, this freak fest can begin

I wanna rub your body down with oil
And get to know your needs
I'll do whatever it takes
To deliver your filthiest fantasies
Let me take your body to the land
Of endless ecstasy
I promise I can show you the way
Just follow me!

Baby this tongue should be a
Legalized licensed weapon
Cause I'm about to sentence that pussy
To some long hours of good licking

Then I'm gone let you ride on this wood
So, you can see what you been missing
Yeah, I can do it any way you want it
But 69 is my favorite position

So, just call me the hammer
Cause tonight I'm gonna be a banger
I swear this dick should come with a sign
That says please beware of the danger

But I'm tired of all this talking
Come and let me extinguish that fire
Cause I wanna know all your fantasies
And your freakiest desires

Baby, playtime is over
So, it's time to let this ride begin
And once you get a taste of this lovin
You'll be cuming again and again
And anytime you want me to stop
Boo, all you gotta do is say when

Yeah, I'll have them legs shaking so hard
That you'll be begging me to stop
No, I'm not like those quick type brothas

I promise I can run out the clock

Yeah, I'm gone bring out that Freak

I'm gone let you ride until you drop!

So, just call me the man of steel

Cause my dick is hard as a rock!

SEXUAL SLAVE

At first, I was afraid
Of my deep sexual rage
But I cast my reservations aside
Allowing me to recognize
That I was denying
The Inner Freak Inside

You didn't care about
The difference in our age
So, I became your sexual slave
You said you wanted my body
So, my body I gave

But there is an image in my brain
Of a memory that remains
As I'm reminded by this spot
Where your semen left a stain

I wonder if you and I will last
Or am I just another piece of ass
I wonder if you'll still desire me
When time has passed

Could you ever be that unkind?
After we made love from behind
I'm trying to fight these
Negative thoughts in my mind
But my fears made me
Hit pause and rewind

Yeah, I remember back
When we first met
And how you said that this was
More than some meaningless sex!
You had my pussy so wet
That moment I'll never forget

How we started fucking and kissing
And the way you had my body twisting
Fuck me harder and harder I kept insisting
And you made me cum so hard
That I felt the room shifting

I know that the sex is lit!
And I love the way he sucks on my clit!
But I told him that I needed a man
Who is ready to commit!
Because I need more than good head

I need to have my soul fed

And if he wasn't ready to give me his pledge

Then I'd have to evict him from my bed

Later we came to a better understanding

About our situation

Because we engaged in a higher

Intimate conversation

He told me that he wanted more

Then physical penetration

So, there was no need for doubts

Or contemplations

He said I never cared about

The difference in our age

So, I'm asking you to be my wife

Not my sexual slave

For a soulmate like you

Is what I've always prayed

And my plan is to be with you

Until the end of my days

MR. KRYPTONITE

Kryptonite is a substance that is known to cause weakness in certain individuals

I thought I was a superwoman

I thought that there was no battle

That I couldn't fight

But that was before the day

I met Mr. Kryptonite

He said hello beautiful queen

How are you doing tonight?

And the way his voice cut into my soul

He could have had me that night

So, you see there was no place I could run

And no place that I could hide

Because it seems that we were two stars

Who were destined to collide

I had never found myself

Feeling so needy

I even agreed to his

friend with benefits treaty

Convincing myself that

I was enough woman for you

And that eventually I would
Make you my boo
And I just assumed that
He knew that too
So, I foolishly settled
For our secret rendezvous

No, I'm not a gambler
But it was my heart that made that bet
And now I was caught up
in a sexual game of Russian Roulette

Now I was enthralled
By this unforeseen scheme
Now I was just his pawn
Until he sacrificed me for the next queen

But I couldn't let you go
Because I was addicted to your thrills
Now you had me so hooked
That my punani percolated at your will
Now I'm getting tired of us
Just being intimate friends
And I want us to have
More than convenient weekends

I dream that one day
We'll walk hand in hand
I dream that one day
I can tell the world
That you are my man

But whenever I try to pull away
You hold me so tight
Killing me softly your Kryptonite
While I cursed all those urges
That I can't seem to fight
Wondering how something so wrong
Can feel so damn right!
So, I continued to stomach you
Because you fed me just enough
To get me through
Keeping me on a strict diet
Of only you!

Yes, you were my weekly feast
And I was like a hungry child
Craving only your sweets
Wanting you more and more
Week, after week
You had me feeling so high

On Saturday and Sunday
That my body was wilted
And hungover by Monday
I was feening for you on
Tuesday and Wednesday
As I crawled into Thursday
Because I needed to feel your touch
In the worse way

You became my dominator
And I was in total submission
Waiting for your arousing permission
Because I couldn't get this addiction
Out of my system

So, I traded my pleasure for pain
Sacrificed my flesh in vain
Just to hear you
Moan my name
And when Friday night came
I was once again yours to tame

Now the anticipation in the air
is oh so sweet
And as our bodies embrace

I'm feverishly lusting for your heat

Slowly you kiss my lips

And I can longer speak

Then the door closes

And into my bedroom we retreat

And then once again

He held me so tight

Killing me softly

With his Kryptonite

I WANT THAT OooooWeeeee

He stood there watching me
As I stared off into space
And I sat there wishing
That I had a better poker face
Because he already knew
That I was hungry for a taste
So, I told him I want that OooooWeeee!

Like veins wanna bleed
Like babies wanna feed
Like addicts growing
Fields of weeds
And Poppy seeds
I said I'd howl at the moon
When you give it to me
Your stroke goes so deep
That My Third Eye wanna peek

I'm sensing his intentions
In the back of my mind
Then I feel my eyes
Starting to roll behind

Because I'm about to fly
On his magic carpet ride
He wanna feel it in my gut
He got me face down and ass up
And my pussy is so wet
Because we about to fuck!

I lay there naked in the dark
My back is perfectly arched
We're fucking so hard
That we're creating a spark
We make love like a team
Kegels help me do my part
And this ain't just about getting a nut
It's about feeling the blood flowing
Through our hearts

We are one like a mixture
He frames my body like a picture
He drinks my elixir
And memorizes my curves like scriptures

He gives me pennies for my thoughts
But already knows what I'm thinking
His lips already knew

What I wanted them to do
I wanted that Oooooo!
I wanted him to make it do what it do!
Smoke up my essence like voodoo!

I want a tongue bath
Soaking me up until I gasp!
I wanna be broke
So, he can fix me
Stand out in the crowd
So, he can pick me
Pour honey on my skin
So, he can lick me

Wind my body up
And watch me tick
Simmer in my gravy
Until it's thick!
He's my magician
He knows the trick
I'm so addicted to his OoooooWeeeee
I think I'm gone need another fix!

☐

I'M SHOOK

Boo your lovin is so damn good!
I'm about to get out this bed
And make dinner for you!
Cause I wanna be
A winner for you!
Shit, I wanna ask Oprah
How I can be a little thinner for you!

Because the way you get under my skin
Our souls must be twins
You're like the Yang to my Yin
That's why I gotta have you
At least once a day
Like my vitamins

And the size of that bone
Be all up in my kill zone
Now I got a love jones
Like Nina Simone
Boo you got my soul consumed
And I be smiling
When you not even in the room

I ain't never felt this way!

And I think what I'm trying to say

Needs be written and produced

Like some big Broadway play

So just give me some direction

And let me know

How you want me to handle

Your erection

Cause you got me shook!

Like some erotica type book

I Love the way that you

Finger my pages

And this story ain't suitable

For all ages

Cause what we do

Is mostly X-rated

Fucking hard

In dark secret places

So, tell your Ex's

You ain't coming back

Cause you just upgraded!

And baby I'm not the type to beg

Nah, I'm the type to lay back

With my ass on the edge

Unfold my legs

Let you give me some head

Then leave a puddle in your bed

Did you hear what I said?

You got me shook!

You got me all twisted up

And now I don't really give a fuck!

Because just the touch of your hands

And my panties drop at your command

So, let all them haters talk

I really don't care

Because I know only you

Can take me there

The way you hold my legs up in the air

Boo we're on deeper level

With the vibe we share

We're like diamonds in the sky

Our connection is so rare

Boo can't you see this love is such a good look

And baby what I'm trying to say is

You got me shook!

THE WOMAN CONNOISSEUR

Listen ladies

The woman connoisseur

Likes them

Smart and educated

But freaky and inflated

Sometimes booty size exaggerated

Hips forceful and wide

With nectar bursting inside

He likes them curvy and ample

Sweetie he needs more than a sample

Them thighs gotta be

Thick and toned

So, you can handle that bone?

He likes them bushy and cushy

Because real men eat pussy!

So, give him a ring

He'll come and make that shit sing

Just let him do the damn thing!

Because he's a connoisseur of women

And he'll answer all of your questions

From sun-kissed to ebony

He adores every complexion

Because you're a stunning masterpiece

And all he can see is your perfection

No matter day or night

He'll give you long-lasting erections

He's all for you sister queen

Cause you got that

Sweet black jellybean!

And that man is just a feen

For your luscious cream

So, whatever you shall desire

He'll cum at your command

But sistah remember,

He melts in your mouth!

Not in your hands?

MY DARK KNIGHT

He is my dark knight
He's amazingly sexy and polite
I swear his lovemaking is so tight
That he makes my body soar
To new heights!

When I feel him pressing against me
With that dynamic bulge his in trunks
I know the scent of my pheromones
Will lead him to exactly what I want

Sometimes we explode with emotions
And we don't always make it to the bed
So, he just lifts me up against the wall
And unleashes some delicious head
His tongue circles and circles around my clit
As I moan and I moan saying yeah that's it!

I get so mesmerized by the perfection
Of his dark chiseled frame
Because there is magic in the way
That his potent jewels swing

Only he has the power to make
My punani flow like the rain
And he never lets me come down
Until I call out his name

Sometimes I slowly kiss him
On his soft full lips
And then I wrap my long legs
Around his muscular hips

Because he loves it when my punani
Begins to flex and grip
As I ride the shit
Out of that black marble dick

And I enjoy the pleasure of swallowing
His thick and mighty shaft
And how my tongue traces his balls
When I wanna make his nut last

We fuck and we fuck
Then we take a little break
Because it's that last fuck of the night
That truly makes my heart palpitate
I know his essence is building

With every inch of him that I take
So, when he asks me how I want it
I say put it on my face

Because my lips are so ready
And I my tongue can't hardly wait
For that delicious moment
When my dark knight ejaculates!

MINDGASMS

Listen,
I got some foreplay
That will make you real wet
And this way more interesting
Then traditional sex

First, I wanna come into your essence
While you ride on the depths of my mind
Let me turn you on to a Mindgasm
I promise it's an orgasm of a different kind

I wanna spread you mind open
I wanna make love to your brain
I wanna cum inside your thoughts
Before I get your punani engaged

So, get ready to vibe on this conversation
And together we can Mindgasm
On to a new elevation
I want you to experience the essence of me
Because a freaky Sapiosexual is what I be

Let me entice you with erotically

Thought provoking communication

And, indulge your imagination

With a new form of intoxication

Then I'll spread your reflections

On my rising projection

And prepare your dimension

For my profound interjection

I want to get off on your contributions

And bathe you with innovative solutions

I wanna let you feast on my inquisitions

And excite you with new positions

Baby I told you this type of foreplay

Was gonna get you real wet

And this way more interesting

Then traditional sex

But first, I gotta come into your essence

While you ride on the depths of my mind

So, I can turn you on to a Mindgasm

I promise it's an orgasm of a different kind

THE
PUNANI
ZONE

SEXY AND GROWN

Girl last night!
He had me so hot on the phone
He had me feeling all sexy and grown!
So, I told him to come over
Because I didn't want to be alone

Then I lit some candles
And put something sexy on
As soon as he walked in
I knew it was about to be on
Because the brotha was hella, hella sexy
And he was wearing that good cologne!

I had on my sexy lingerie
That hot pink chiffon
And he was drooling on my tits
Like he was a fresh newborn

Girl I knew we was gonna fuck
From dusk till dawn
When he started feasting my yum-yum
Like it was a filet minion

I swear he had my punani
Ready and wet at the drop zone
I swear he licked me so good
I melted like an Ice cream cone

Then, I went down on my knees
As I stretched my jawbone
Then I grabbed that dick
And went to work on that wishbone

Oooh he was hard as rhinestones
I gave him head so deep
He thought his shit was gone
He said it felt like heaven
The way I was killing that dome

I swallowed that delicious nut
And five minutes later he was back full grown
He said my punani was so good
He just couldn't leave it alone!

So, we came multiple times
Switching our positions like time zones
He held my legs on his shoulders
And I was flexing my hipbones

He went so deep
He hit blew out my backbone
Swinging that thang
Like he was playing a trombone!

But, oh when he hit that spot
Girl my mind was blown!
And it sounded like music
Cause we both started to moan

Then he held me in his arms
And said daddy's home!
Girl, last night we was feeling sexy and grown!
So sexy and grown!

THE HONEYMOON

It was their honeymoon night
And it was time for some serious lovemaking
They paused and stared into each other's eyes
Knowing that this night was going to be amazing
She knew that dick was ready to stand
And her pussy was fervently waiting
Because tonight was gonna be wild
And this sex was gonna be back breaking

The reception was over
And now it was time for bed
Because tonight was a celebration
Of these two horny ass newlyweds

There would be no holding back
Both of their desires were going to be met
It was time to unleash their inner freak
And time for some soul snatching sex

He tongue fucked her punani
While holding up both of her legs
And she came inside his mouth

While she ran her fingers through his dreads

He kissed her from head to toe
Then he gently slid inside her
She ran her fingers up and down his spine
As her yoni gripped him tighter

She took in every inch of him
Then said "Baby come on let's switch"
So, he turned over on his back
And she went Kamasutra on that dick

Together they move in rhythm
While he firmly squeezed her ass
And she rode his dick so well
He almost caught some whiplash

He moaned damn I'm so lucky
To have you as my wife
He said this punani is my new home
And I plan to cum in it every night

He said I want your body and your mind
And I love how your soul speaks to mine
Your beauty goes deeper than you know

That's why you are truly one of a kind

He knew her appetite was ferocious
Seemed like she was never truly done
She loved it in every position
And he enjoyed the privilege of making her cum

She said baby can you rub on my clit
So, that I can really get a good nut
And I want you to give me all that dick
I wanna feel you in my gut

Then when the night was over
He said baby was it good for you?
She said it was the best day of my life
And that dick was perfect boo!

ANTICIPATING

As the blazing sun settles
And the cool moon kisses her skin
Anxiously she squeezes her thighs
Anticipating the sensual rising within

Her nipples are soft and tender
And her punani is sultry and wet
So, she begins exploring her body
To relieve that burdening stress

She reaches for her feel-good thing
And starts thrusting it deep inside her abyss
As the other part of her toy
Pleasingly vibrated on top of her wet clit

Then she opened her legs
Into a very comfortable state
While she continues to guide her toy
In and around her intimate space

She doesn't want to cum too fast
So, she slows down her pace

Relishing every minute of this ecstasy
With a look of bliss all over her face

She deliberately moves her punani
In a slow winding motion
While generously pleasuring herself
And enjoying the deepness of her stroking

The vibration on her clit
Is now filling her body with a flood of passion
As she's feeding her throbbing pussy
With the utmost satisfaction

With joy she calls out
Because her nectar is leaking
As the euphoria builds up
Oh, how she is gloriously peaking!

Because she's satisfying her needs
Even if there is no man in her world
Oh, how she shivers
As her toes begin to curl!

The sensations take over her body
And the sensual moon kisses her skin

Yet joyfully she waits
Anticipating the sensual rising within

CAPTURING HIS ESSENCE

He said that her hands were truly magnificent
And they had to be touched by magic
Because every stroke she's giving him
Feels so blissful and orgasmic

He said only she had the power
To conduct his long and thick shaft
And it was as if she was his very own
Sensual lightning staff

He said no one else knows how
To fully capture his essence
And that her level of skills
Was his most fortunate blessing

But she was also aroused
By his body's full submission
As she skillfully stroked on his shaft
Because capturing his essence
Was her favorite mission

His swollen rod joyfully obeyed her

And her commanding grip gladly obliged him
As all his needs were being met
By the euphoria building up inside him

He moaned and moaned
Asking her to let his milky sap pour out
He said darling release my nectar
I want to cum in your warm and supple mouth

His moans made her wet
Because she could feel her walls secreting
But she also enjoyed making him wait
Because she liked to keep him pleading

His body started trembling
As she released his delicious cream
Then she slowly licked around the head
And began sucking up his glorious stream

He said those hands are so magnificent
They must be touched by some kind of magic
Because every stroke you gave me
Felt so blissfully orgasmic

He said only you have the power

To conduct my long and thick shaft
And I love the way you devoured my nectar
It's like you're my sensual lightning staff

He said no one else knows how
To fully capture my essence
And sweetheart your level of skills
Has truly been my most fortunate blessing!

RIDEM COWGIRL

You think you can handle this beautiful ass?
She said with a wink and a smile
Cause I'm gonna throw this fat punani
For a good long while
So, getty-up Big John
Cause I'm going for the record-breaking mile
Yeah, tonight I'm riding that dick
In reverse cowgirl style!

So, let me saddle up
Watch me slay that dick right
John you ain't ready for this punani
Boy I'm gonna have you sprung tonight
Yeah, I'm getting on top
And I'm in full command
So, boo whatever you do
Your dick better stand!
Cause I'm about to bounce on that pole
With no fucking hands!
Like I'm the hard riding Lone Ranger
And you're that sexy bad man!

Cause tonight I want it real rough
So, I need you to keep that dick up
Big John I'm not playing
I want you to hold that nut!
Yeah, I got plenty of beer to drink
It's inside the cooler in my truck
So, come on big John?
Cause it's time to Rodeo Fuck

Now let me fill your mouth
With these double-d tits!
Hold that nut Big John
I'm not done ridding that dick

Come and get this punani
Let me see you get buck wild
I wanna see you swing that dick
And make this night worth my while

Now hold on with both hands
She said with a wink and a smile
Cause tonight I'm riding that dick
In reverse cowgirl style!

THAT DUDE

Nah, not that dude!
Cause he's snack food
And I need a full course meal
Not some fast food
But you see that dude
He's got my back dude
He keeps my body on track dude
Because the way he hit it
I gotta throw it back dude!

Yeah he's that dude!
Always polite and never rude
And knows how to put me in a sexy mood
He keeps my punani pleasantly subdued
Because he moves my body like rhythm and blues

Yeah, he's that keep it 100 dude
That I'm for real dude
He's got great sex appeal dude
And really cares about how I feel dude

Because man that dude -

He makes me wanna stay nude
The blow out my back dude!
Feast on my body like food
But still hit me right back dude!
Yeah that dude!

And he doesn't just talk about it
He shows and proves
He answers all my calls
He takes me to the mall
He makes me climb the walls
He makes me wanna give it all!
Because he's that -
Fully equipped dude
Make me strip dude
Suck on my clit dude
And he never, ever, ever
Cums too quick dude!
Because he's got that good shit dude!

But yeah that dude -
He might be a little hood
But he still makes sure we're good
Before he lays down that wood
And the vibes are already understood

Because he makes me cum
Like a black queen should!

And that dude –
He doesn't gossip
He keeps our shit confidential
Not too complex
He likes to keep shit simple
He's real organic
Ain't nothing about him artificial
Very intuitive
The way he picks up on my signals
And he really knows how
To make my tea pot whistle
Have my punani squirting like a pistol
Cause when he gives me that dick it's official!
And he's physically and mentally beneficial
Like those Chakra Crystals

Listen man
That dude -
He makes me laugh
He's got jokes
He surprises me
With love notes

And feeds my mind

With conscious quotes

Yeah, sometimes we blaze

On that good smoke

Before he slays me

With that deep stroke

His dick is so good

It feels like I got the holy ghost!

But then I hit him back

With that deep throat

Man, that brotha gives me hope!

That's why we still growing

Even though he be knowing

That dick he be throwing

Is mind blowing

Leaving my punani swollen

But our thoughts stay connected

Like a semi-colon

So, we take our time

Yeah, we just be strolling

Cause his type is easy going

Hands holding

Marriage proposing

While them others dude

Just be scrolling…

Cause, that dude -

Man, he kills my pain like ibuprofen

He's respectful but outspoken

His mind's focused

And he ain't looking for some easy open

That's why he's one of the few chosen

So nah, not that dude

Cause he's just snack food

And I need a full course meal

Not some fast food

But you see that dude

He's got my back dude

He keeps my body on track dude

Because the way he hit it

I gotta throw it back dude!

PUNANI PLAYDATES

I NEED A FREAK

I need a Super Freak
One who knows how to treat me
And knows how to eat me
One who knows how to slang
That delicious meat
One who will hit it from the back
As he spreads my cheeks
One who will make the whole bed squeak
And won't stop licking
Until my nut is complete

A freak who can take me there
One who needs my pussy
Like he needs the air
Goes down on his knees
To say a quick prayer
Before he tastes me everywhere
One who can make me cum
With the tip of his tongue
Then flip me on my side
And beat it like a drum
Have me totally sprung

By the time he's done

One that can put my body to the test
Suck on my nipples
And massage my breasts
Cause I want a freak who's
Thick, long and stays erect
Grabs me by the back of my neck
And strokes me
Until I give that dick
The proper respect
Yeah, I need a Freak
With a Capital "F" on his Chest
His dimensions be so long
He should be under arrest

I want him to fill me with his elixir
While we play naked twister
And if he wants to have a 3 way
Then we can add another sister

I wanna slide down on his slippery slope
I wanna skip on that dick like I'm jumping rope
Let him quench my thirst like a frosty Coke
Then I finish him off in the back of my throat

I wanna be the only one he craves

Fuck him in one hundred and one

Different ways

While moans my name

Let my essence run through his veins

Fuck him through the night

And uplift him through the days

Cause I want a freak I can love

All the way to his grave

One that I can roll with

Endure and grow old with

On bad days I can console with

Open my soul with

Make goals with

And build a home with

So, give me a Super Freak

One who knows how to treat me

And knows how to eat me

One who knows how to slang

That delicious meat

One who will hit it from the back

As he spreads my cheeks

One who will make the whole bed squeak

And won't stop licking

Until my nut is complete

WANTING HIM

I laid there waiting for him
My body was lusting for him
My hormones were going crazy for him
My mouth was salivating
I think I had drool on my chin
I could almost melt at the sight of
his coco brown skin
He had my punani flexing
Like a muscle at the gym
Cause the way he licked his lips
With that sexy ass grin
Made me wanna swallow him whole
And just let him fall right in

All I wanna worship is his phallus
Because I ain't worried about a Sin
I wanna let the harmony of his dick
Conduct my punani like a Hymn

I want our bodies to share a language
That only we know how to speak
Twist my spine in the right position

So, he can make my G-Spot squeak

I want him to enter my domain
Bust right through my thighs
I want him to extinguish my fire
I want him to make me cum alive

I wanna get lost in the moment
I wanna close my eyes
I wanna share a 69
So, we can suck each other dry
Because there's nothing more delicious
than the meat on his bone
And nothing sounds sweeter
Then the deepness of his moan
Because our bedroom is the place
We call the erotic zone
Where he takes me to heaven
And calls my body his home

Because he makes my heart race
When he starts to say his grace
And I know he's gone to clean his plate
When I drop that punani on his face

That's why I'll wait for him

And I be lusting for him

Cause my hormones

Be going crazy for him

And sometimes I get a little

Drool on my chin

And I almost melt at the sight

Of his coco brown skin

Cause he makes my punani start flexing

Like a muscle at the gym

And the way he licks his lips

With that sexy ass grin

Makes me wanna swallow him whole

And just let him fall right in

G-SPOT

Yeah, I can tell you're the type
That like them kisses down low
You wanna ride on my face
And leave me begging for mo'
But this dick is a weapon
In case you didn't know
So, let me give you these strokes
Real nice and slow

Yeah, I wanna see them panties drop
Cause I know that punani
Is getting wet as a mop
Yeah, that pussy is gone be mines
Once I stroke that g-spot

You see my dick is a serious addiction
And this long ass anaconda
Will have you walking like an ancient Egyptian
I'll have them legs more confused
Then a clear contradiction
I'll be beating up that yoni
Like a drumming competition

So, let me give you this deepness
Let me be your big dirty secret
Cause all I'm trying to do
Is release your sweetness

I wanna feel your rain
Let you ride my dick like a train
Then let me slide it in your mouth
So, you can lick the sugar off this cane

I can see how bad you want it
So, don't trip
I know you want this good dick
Cause you know a brotha like me
Don't ever cum too quick

And I'm gonna dive in deeper
Then a torpedo submarine
I'm gone be directing that pussy
Like a porno scene

Ain't no need to fantasize
Cause baby I got the perfect size
So, cum and sit on daddy's lap
And let me take you for ride

Let me see you arch your back

Lord have mercy that ass is fat!

Yeah hold it hit just like that

While I take it to the hole like Shaq

You can moan and howl

But it's too late to call a foul

Yeah, I'm dicking this punani down

Cause this is my domain now

Yeah, I knew you was the type

That liked them kisses down low

I knew you wanted to ride my face

And leave me begging for mo'

I told you my dick is a weapon

So now you know

That's why I gave you them long strokes

Real nice and slow

I told you them panties was gonna drop

And I knew that punani was

getting wet as a mop

And I knew that pussy was gone be mine

Once I found that g-spot

BLACK OASIS

Sometimes I just chill like a lioness in the den
But sometimes I go out and prowl
On some of these fine ass men

And sometimes I feel like
I'm in the middle of an Oasis
When I'm walking by seeing
All them beautiful black faces

I like his butter pecan
And I like his mahogany tan
But I wanna taste his honey raw
Cause I'm really feeling
That sexy goatee around his jaw
But I wanna feel the rush
Of his dark expresso
While I'm running my fingers
Through that fresh cut afro

But I like that brotha's dreadlocks
And that brotha got some curly kinks
I'm getting so aroused by this Black Oasis

But I need to find me a real African Mandink

I wanna find myself a King
So, he can plant his seeds
Because I want to be his peace
I want to be all that he needs

I want to cleanse his aura
With some burning sage
Then I wanna fulfill his desires
And release his sexual rage

I wanna let him feast on my body
And let him taste my mind
I wanna tap into his energy
And let our souls combine

I wanna align with his cells
I wanna ride him well
I wanna get lost his moans
I want him to make my punani his home

I wanna lose control
When he looks into my eyes
I wanna give him some head

Before he slides inside
I wanna feel his strength
And his size
I wanna let him go so deep
That I can't help but cry

I wanna swim in his chocolate pool
I wanna give him these jewels
I wanna meditate on his dick
Like it's a spiritual tool

I wanna get drunk on his stream
I wanna give him this sweet nectarine
So, that he can feast on my punani
And make me cum like Queen

INVITED

Now I know I called to invite you
But first let me tease and entice you
Because I wanna mentally to please you
Before I sexually relieve you
Now don't be so apprehensive
My time is valuable but not expensive
I'm confident that you'll enjoy
The quality of this wood
And I know you'll be back
If I stroke it good

So, let me lick, suck and salivate
We don't have to fuck
I can watch you masturbate
And save my sperm
Until you're ready to procreate
But give me a second
And I can cum too
You see all I really need
Is the view of you
Now take some of this protein
And let me rub it on your lips

I think you gone have twins
With those childbearing hips

Baby you don't have to moan for me
Unless you really mean it
Because I know the harder you cum
The more you gone feen it

So, let me sprinkle all my seeds
And pull out all these weeds
Baby just enjoy this summer breeze
While you go down on your knees

I just wanna saturate your soil
Because you are my earth
And your body is so fertile and prime
So prime for giving birth

My Queen together we shall lay
And our seeds will be born
Then our cipher will be complete
And we shall both live on!

SEXUAL BEAST

A Sistah as fine as you
Don't have to be alone on any night
Just slide by my crib
And let me do you right
I've got the elixir that you need
I'll leave you weak in the knees
Cause I'm that elite type of freak
That's why they call me the sexual beast

You'll find that I'm
Skillfully trained
To impart the perfect amount of
Pleasure and pain
I'm about to show and prove
So, there's no need for me to explain

I'll start with some
Kissing and hugging
And maybe a little toe sucking
Give that clit a good rubbing
Then get ready for
A whole lot of fucking

Cause I'm lean and hard
And my dick is super charged
And when I give you this yard
You gone be screaming for god

I love the way you blush
But it's time to hold them legs up
Please believe and trust
That I'm about to get up in that gut

There are so many ways
For us to fuck
And I got all night to bust
But first I wanna make you nut
So, I can lick that punani up

Baby, you see how my dick can swing
That's how you know I'm a King
And fucking ain't just something I do
Baby fucking is my thing

I got that hypnotic dick
I'll make love to your cranium
So, baby welcome to Wakanda
Now cum and get this Vibranium

Watch me make that pussy twerk
While I'm putting in this work
Yeah, I might be a sexual beast
But I still let the ladies cum first
So, baby hold on to my dreads
Cause I'm about to put a dent in this bed
I'm gone slay that pussy till you sleep
Exactly like I said

Yeah, I'm too nasty to be a Christian
So, just call me your climax technician
I'll fuck you in every position
And bring your orgasms into fruition

Baby it's all about technique
See I told you I was a freak
But I think you had enough of this meat
So, I'll holla at you again next week

Because you're my favorite type of honey
And yes, that pussy was very yummy
You gave my dick a run for his money
But I can see you're walking kinda funny

So, just give me a call

And I'll cum and stroke you

Through the night

Just bring that pussy to me

And let me do you right

Cause I've got the elixir that you need

Baby I'll leave you weak in the knees

Because I'm that elite type of freak

And that's why they call me

The sexual beast!

THE-HIT-IT-MAN

Better think before you surrender
Better take a good notice of where you stand
Girl you better heed this warning
Before you lay with the-hit-it-man

He's a punani tracker
A smooth kind of player
He's a cunning carnivore
And a merciless pussy slayer

He knows how to make you laugh
And he knows exactly what you like
Because he only needs one chance
To lay down that golden pipe

He can speak in different dialects
I think he's Bilingual
He will flatter you with beautiful compliments
This man really knows how to
Conversate and mingle

He knows how to find the ladies

Who are attractive, horny and single
And he's very good at finding your spot
So, he can make that punani tingle
He keeps his body in impeccable shape
You can see it through his tight-fitting tees
And after about two drinks or maybe three
He'll whisper a customary plea
Would like to spend the night with me?
He'll ask with one hand sliding up your knee

He always paces himself
He never makes a move too fast
Teasing them with his beautiful lips
And his deep and sexy laugh

He never wants a quickie
He wants to make it last
So, he may entice you with some rose
Petals In a warm and relaxing bath

He's flawless at feeding you lines
Yes, he'll even show you a good time
Candlelight with dinner and wine
You'll be like putty in his hands
Because his chocolate ass is so fine

He has all kinds of intimate ploys
He's an artist at bringing women joy
He'll fuck them good with his sex toys
So that he can get them ready for his big boy

Sometimes he'll slowly use his fingers
To arouse you with pleasure and pain
Then he'll kiss you from head to toe
And make you call out his name

He'll say you taste like candy
As he savors your sweet flesh
He'll say, "I just want to love you
You'll see I'm not like the rest"

He'll tell you not to worry
And that he will always be down
But he only wants one night
And has no intentions on
staying around

And after that one last stroke
He'll whisper, "I almost feel like I'm your man
But my heart's just not ready for love
So, baby I hope you understand"

He'll say, "but one of these days
I'll come back and I'll make you mine"
That's when the tears will begin to flow
From your heartbroken eyes

Because you gave him your love
But all he gave you were lies
You'll try to convince him
You'll try to change his mind
And he'll give you a forehead kiss
And tell you not to cry
Saying he'll be back one day
But for now, my love this is goodbye

So, ladies please think before you surrender
Remember take a good notice
Of where you stand
And I hope you all heed this warning
Before you lay with the-hit-it-man

SOME NIGHTS

Some nights I put away my pride
And pick up the phone!
Some nights I might have to call
Brotha Tyrone!
Cause it ain't hardly easy sleeping alone
And some nights I gotta have
That goodnight Bone!

I wanna feel the sultry sweat
From our bodies
Bleeding into those cool cotton sheets
I wanna feel his hands tracing
Down my spine
Before he cups both of my ass cheeks

Cause tonight, I have an itch
That I really need him to reach
Tonight, he can bend me over
And fuck this punani balls deep

I'll put my legs on his shoulders
And let him wear this punani out

I'll smile when he hands me a pillow
So that I can scream and shout

I want him to eat me with a spoon
And tell me that I'm yummy
Then flip me over on my tummy
So, he can get all this honey

I swear this Brotha deserves
The Unforgettable Dick Award
Because he always kills it
When I give him these drawers
He knows how to takes charge
He told me to down on all fours
So that he can make me cum harder
Then the time before

But that's not all
Because he ain't through
That was just round one
And tonight, we gone need at least two

Yeah it was that kind of night
That's why I had to pick up the phone
Tonight, I had put my pride to the side

and call Brotha Tyrone

Cause it ain't hardly easy sleeping alone

And some nights, I gotta have

that goodnight Bone!

Keep In Touch With
The Author:

amazon.com/author/sharrantaylor

FB Page: Author Kween Yakini

FB Page: The Erotic Poetress

IG Page: @eroticpoetress

YouTube: Kween Yakini's Poetry

Email :   authorkweenyakini@gmail.com

Please turn to the next page to enjoy a preview poem that will be in my next book…

BOOK PREVIEW

BROOKLYN QUEEN

Yeah, that city scene

Was anything but serene

But it sure was perfect

For the makings

Of a Brooklyn Queen

Cause here we be strong

But here we be humble

Sometimes we rise

And sometimes we stumble

But you can't let them see you slip

When you're living in these bricks

Cause we go toe to toe

When we throw them fists

We got a few patches of grass

And some benches for old folks to sit

In a jungle of concrete walls

Surrounded by red bricks

And every block looks just like this

So, it doesn't really matter

Just take your pick

Now I know they got plenty of fish in the sea
But they only made one as peculiar as me
That's why them old souls blew in
On an ancient breeze
And gave this gifted child
The wisdom to see

They told me not to be defeated
They gave me the instincts that I needed
Them Ancestors always got my back
They come through like the wind
If they sense any kind of attack

They helped to heal my aching bones
When life hit me with merciless stones
They saw determination in my eyes
And told me to look to the sky
When I need to cry

They taught to me to meditate
To keep my spirits higher
The pulled me back
When I got to close to the fire

They said I was a divine orphan child

Who was left alone to fend

But that I had a broken spirit

That they're intending to mend

Yeah, I was born and raised

On concrete playgrounds

Where big city buses

Helped me to get around

No, I ain't never been afraid

To walk at night

And I ain't never been afraid

to put up a good fight

Cause I'm always protected

By those comforting streetlights

That always led the way

As if they understood my plight

But them ancestral stars

Do more than glisten

They shined down upon me

When my parents went missing

I know them kin folks can hear me

When I be wishing

They say hush don't worry
This is just a temporary condition

So, I look up to the stars
For an extra flare
Cause their spiritual energy
Tells me when to beware

That's why I'm blessed
Because I know somebody cares
But I think it's time to go home
Cause I'm sensing danger over there

I'm always hearing random gun shots
But I hardly ever see any city cops
So, I'll just keep looking for the signs
On these cold city blocks

Yeah, that city scene
Was anything but serene
But it sure was perfect
For the makings
Of a Brooklyn Queen

ABOUT THE AUTHOR

I am truly a humble woman who one day realized that she had a powerful voice inside, and then I found the courage to share it through my poetry. As a poet, I often write about my desires and my experiences because it is the journey that makes who we are. I know that there are others who also have vibrant stories of their own to tell, and my hope is that by sharing mines I have inspired others to one day tell theirs. My personal goal as a writer is to always speak from the heart no matter what the topic of discussion. For me writing is like sharing my own recipe for healing the soul with my readers. I'm grateful to have discovered my true passion for writing, and I will continue to write for as long as I have something that I need to say.

Please leave a review on Author's Amazon Page

amazon.com/author/sharrantaylor

Thank you for reading
"Ode To The Punani"

www.ingramcontent.com/pod-product-compliance
Lightning Source LLC
Chambersburg PA
CBHW020908090426
42736CB00008B/539